MW00562845

ROYAL
HYDERABADI
COOKING

SANJEEV KAPOOR
HARPAL SINGH SOKHI

ROYAL HYDERABADI COOKING

IN ASSOCIATION WITH ALYONA KAPOOR

www.popularprakashan.com

POPULAR PRAKASHAN PVT. LTD.
301, Mahalaxmi Chambers
22, Bhulabhai Desai Road
Mumbai 400 026

(4121)
ISBN 978-81-7991-373-4

Design: Gopi Kukde
Photography: Bharat Bhirangi

PRINTED IN INDIA
by Batra Art Press
A-41, Naraina, Phase-2,
New Delhi

Published by Ramdas Bhatkal
for Popular Prakashan Pvt. Ltd.
301, Mahalaxmi Chambers
22, Bhulabhai Desai Road
Mumbai 400 026

AUTHORS' NOTES

My gastronomical journey exploring the cuisines of India is a continuous one. This time the stop is at Hyderabad, where they say the best food comes with fursat (leisure) and mohabbat (love). A saying which is after my own heart, because I firmly believe that cooking should be done with a lot of love thrown in.

At the very outset, I would especially like to acknowledge my co-author, my old friend and associate Chef Harpal Singh Sokhi's efforts, his dedication and his research that have added new dimensions to this book.

This presentation of the culinary legacy of the Moghuls will enable you to master the art of Hyderabadi cooking because in its pages lies the proof that Hyderabadi food is not just biryani and haleem or baghare baingan and tamatar ka khut. The repertoire is rich and vast, both in vegetarian and non-vegetarian fare. What also distinguishes Hyderabadi food is its sourness… clearly a Telugu influence. Souring enhances the taste of the food and is said to be good the heart and for digestion. Hyderabadi food can also be hot and spicy, again a South Indian or rather Telugu influence. The sting of the red chilli and the bite of the black peppercorn are what distinguishes Hyderabadi cuisine from North Indian cuisine and gives it its own irresistible personality.

As you plan your grand and royal Hyderabadi meal, remember that all recipes are meant to serve four people. We have also kept in mind that there are other complementary dishes in the meal. So go ahead, just turn the pages and get transported to a precious culinary and cultural experience.

As I begin to pen this little note for my first-ever cookbook Royal Hyderabadi Cooking - it is befitting that I express my heartfelt gratitude to my mentor Master Chef Sanjeev Kapoor, who has made it possible for my dream to come true. His guidance and support have not only made this book happen, but have given me new vision for the future.

I am indebted to many close associates and culinary experts whom I have interacted with in all my years of learning. It is rather difficult to mention all the names here, but my sincere thanks to Ustad Habib Pasha under whose guidance I have learnt the art of cooking authentic Hyderabadi food. Begum Mumtaz Khan, an authority in Hyderabadi cuisine, has further helped me in enhancing my knowledge. I am deeply indebted to her too.

I dedicate this book to my parents and my wife Aparna who have always supported me in my endeavours. And of course, to our two little angels, Anushka and Antara who are my best critics.

So without any delay, spread out a royal Hyderabadi dastarkhwan: Boote ke Samose, Murtabak, Mirchi ka Salan, Haleem, Thikri ki Dal, Qaabooli and Sheermal and add a touch of gratifying sweetness with Double ka Meetha and Gil-e-firdaus.

There are other smooth creamy dishes also awaiting your pleasure: refined curries, tender kababs and unforgettable desserts. I am sure that like me, you will develop a passionate fondness for Hyderabadi food!

Harpal S. Sokhi

Revival of a royal art

Say 'Hyderabadi food' and one thought comes to mind: a feudal lifestyle and a lavish cuisine that is rich and painstakingly laborious. Be it the kababs, the kormas or the biryanis, it all entails many hours of marination, fine grinding and slow cooking. But what saddens one is that all this delicious fare is no longer easy to find. The nihari at five o'clock in the morning sold by the roadside; the kabab roti at Machli Kaman at Charminar; the potli masala from Lad Bazar, and the spices from Afzal Gunj, are indeed sweet memories. Today, while authentic Hyderabadi food is still cooked in some homes, and served occasionally at weddings, the art of leisurely cooking is dying. My aim in this book is to revive that art. So when you prepare Paneer Tamatar ka Khut, Mirchi ka Salan and Thikri ki Dal, remember that they represent the legacy of a bygone royal era, when food was king!

Gourmands since forever

The Hyderabadis are great gourmands and very passionate about their food. They eat to satisfy their palates rather than for survival. It is often remarked that Hyderabadis live to eat! Their love affair with food began centuries ago. Not many know that the flag of the earlier Hyderabad State actually had a kulcha (bread) embroidered on it. The story goes that the first Nizam, Asaf Jah I, was asked by Emperor Aurangzeb to move from Delhi to Hyderabad. Before leaving Delhi, Asaf Jah went to seek the blessings of Hazrat Aulia who invited him to share his meal. As time was short, Asaf Jah took a bite of a kulcha and gratefully accepted to carry seven more of the loaves for the journey. They were wrapped in a yellow cloth and Hazrat blessed him with the words "You and your descendents will rule the Deccan for seven generations." Asaf Jah selected a yellow flag for his State of Hyderabad (similar to the cloth which bore the blessed kulchas) proudly embroidered in gold with his headdress and below it the kulcha! And the prophecy of Hazrat came true… the Asaf Jahi Dynasty ruled Hyderabad for seven generations.

A taste of multiculturalism

Hyderabadi food has its own distinct identity, a unique taste and exceptional flavour. It is a blend of the cultural traditions of the North with the sauce and spice of the South and is a true-blue example of cross-cultural interaction. It is the meeting point of rich Moghlai cuisine symbolized by almonds, saffron and khoya and local condiments like coconut, tamarind and green chilli.

In other words, it represents the multicultural and secular nature of its population. The food like the language - a Hyderabadi version of Urdu - is a harmonious mingling of Persian, Arabic,

ABOUT HYDERABADI CUISINE

Telugu and a smattering of Marathi. Some dishes are common to all the communities which have made Hyderabad their home, testifying to the camaraderie between the people. Yet one can find subtle differences of the tastes, the dishes cooked in a Muslim home, a Hindu home or a Parsi home. But then even within one community each family has its own special identity. And this only adds to the variety.

The characters of the cuisine

As you explore Hyderabadi cuisine, you will discover that the single most important distinguishing factor of Hyderabadi food is its sourness - definitely an Andhra influence. Sourness not only adds to the taste of the food, it is also good for the heart and digestion. There is a variety of souring ingredients used in this cuisine such as chigur (tamarind shoots), green and ripe tamarind, ambada leaves, lemons, green mango, dried mango powder, karonda, tomatoes, yogurt, and pomegranate. There was a time when the use of the souring agent reflected a person's status: chigur used by the lower middle class, lemon by the middle class, green mango by the upper middle class and grapes or pomegranate by the affluent. But thankfully this class discrimination no longer exists and people use one or the other souring agent according to taste. Then again, the vaids prescribe that one should never use two different types of souring agents in a single dish. However, in Hyderabadi cuisine this norm does not apply. This is mainly because the climate is excessively dry, and the souring ingredients are good for rehydration. They are used not only in marination but also added to the gravy. Another good thing about the sourness, is that one can go easy on the salt and this is especially good for those who suffer from hypertension. A good tip for the health-conscious of today!

There is a mistaken notion that Hyderabadi food is all about non-vegetarian food. This probably stems from the popularity of nihari with naan for breakfast! Then there is the quintessential haleem that is associated with Hyderabadi food. Indeed their non-vegetarian repertoire is rich and vast, but so is the array of vegetarian dishes. In fact the local Hindus refrain from non-vegetarian food during festivals and even the Shia Muslims avoid non-vegetarian food during Mohurrum. Their pickles and chutneys are famous and many of the dishes like Mirchi ka Salan take on a pickle-like flavour. They cook their dals in a variety of ways each one tastier than the other. Legend has it that a nobleman, Maharaja Sir Kishen Pershad, who enjoyed cooking, could prepare dal in fifty-two different ways!

Learning from the experts

Authentic Hyderabadi food does require time and energy to prepare. And if you go hunting for it in restaurants you will be sorely disappointed. Some five star hotels do serve exceptional fare but that is not accessible to all. The recipes given in this book are a part of the legacy passed on by Ustad Habib Pasha and Begum Mumtaz Khan.

Begum Mumtaz Khan is a living legend. She belongs to the Jagirdhar families of the last Nizam and has actually tasted the food cooked in the royal kitchens. Until a few years ago, she was one of the few people who conducted cooking classes on Hyderabadi cuisine. She has also held many a Hyderabadi food festival in hotels across the globe.

Ustad Habib Pasha is a passionate cook. He has worked his way up the ranks in Hyderabad's famous restaurants. Habib is the one person who has actually revealed to me the various blends of aromatic herbs used in cooking and their uses. It is he who has repeatedly told me that 'Biryani is a process and cannot be mastered in one day'.

When you learn the art from experts, you pick up the tiny nuances of authentic cooking, the secrets of the recipes and then the final blessing of being able to cook just like them. It is from them I learned that the dough for lukmi should not be worked upon too much. The oil for frying them has to be heated on a low heat, before the lukmis are added, with the heat being increased only towards the end of the frying time. Another tip: while making murtabak ensure that the mutton is minced really fine. You can also make a Puran Murtabak replacing the savoury stuffing with a sweet chana dal stuffing enriched with saffron, pistachios, almonds, khoya and cardamoms. Who would have thought that adding a few strands of fresh dill or fenugreek to a vegetable biryani would elevate it to newer heights? Or that one should use only khada masala as powdered spices subdue the flavour of the dish. I also learnt that potli masala need not actually be tied up in a bundle. One can boil the ingredients in water, reduce the decoction, then strain and use the flavoured water for cooking.

It is these little touches that differentiate the ordinary recipe from that in an expert's diary. I do hope that as I share these secrets, the food that comes to your table is reminiscent of the erstwhile royal kingdom of Hyderabad.

Harpal S. Sokhi

CONTENTS

BADAM SHORBA

'Shorba' is a poetic word for soup. And this recipe, with the creaminess of almonds, forms a poetic combination of taste and nutrients.

Ingredients

175 grams almonds (badam)
2 teaspoons butter
1¼ teaspoons refined flour (maida)
1 cup milk

½ teaspoon sugar
salt to taste
¼ teaspoon white pepper powder
1½ tablespoons cream

Method

•   Soak the almonds in hot water for a few minutes. Drain and peel. Slice ten or twelve almonds for garnishing and grind the rest to a smooth paste.

•   Melt the butter in a pan; add the flour and sauté for one minute. Gradually pour in the milk stirring continuously to prevent lumps from forming. Add the sugar, salt and white pepper powder and cook, stirring continuously, till the mixture comes to a boil. Lower the heat and simmer for five minutes, stirring occasionally.

•   Add the almond paste and two cups of hot water and simmer for ten to fifteen minutes, stirring occasionally, till the soup thickens.

•   Toast the sliced almonds. Sprinkle the toasted almonds and drizzle the cream over the soup just before serving piping hot.

SABZI KA SHORBA

Being creative with vegetables is the hallmark of a Hyderabadi cook. Who would imagine that the base of this aromatic soup is the humble lauki?

Ingredients

3 medium potatoes, cut into ½-inch cubes
3 large tomatoes, chopped
100 grams bottle gourd (doodhi/lauki),
  cut into ½-inch cubes
2 tablespoons oil
5-6 black peppercorns
2 cloves
2 onions, chopped
2 garlic cloves, crushed

1 inch ginger, chopped
3 cups vegetable stock
¼ teaspoon turmeric powder
salt to taste
½ teaspoon sugar
½ teaspoon black pepper powder
1 tablespoon lemon juice
1 spring onion, chopped

Method

• Heat the oil in a deep pan; add the peppercorns and cloves and sauté for half a minute. Add the onions and cook over medium heat till translucent. Add the garlic and ginger and stir. Add the potatoes, tomatoes and bottle gourd and cook over medium heat for five minutes, stirring occasionally.

• Add the vegetable stock, turmeric powder, salt, sugar and pepper powder. Increase the heat and bring the soup to a boil. Lower the heat and simmer for about thirty minutes, or till the vegetables are tender. Cool and purée in a blender. Pass the purée through a strainer.

• Return the purée to the pan, add the lemon juice, and bring the soup to a boil. Serve hot, garnished with chopped spring onion.

ALOO KE GARLAY

This is an ostentatious version of the ever popular batata wada. So what if the process is a bit tedious... the final flavour is unique!

Ingredients

6 medium potatoes, boiled and mashed
1 cup + 3 tablespoons gram flour (besan)
salt to taste
¼ teaspoon red chilli powder
2 tablespoons oil + for deep-frying
1 medium onion, chopped
1 teaspoon ginger paste
1 teaspoon garlic paste
a pinch of turmeric powder
2 tablespoons chopped fresh coriander
  leaves
5-6 fresh mint leaves, chopped
2 green chillies, chopped
1 tablespoon lemon juice
3 tablespoons cornflour
a pinch of baking powder

Method

•   Mix together one cup of gram flour, salt and half the chilli powder in a bowl. Add water and knead into a soft dough. Take one tablespoon of dough and shape into a ball. Form similar balls with the rest of the dough. Heat the oil in a kadai; deep-fry the balls of dough till golden. Drain on absorbent paper.

•   Heat two tablespoons of oil in a pan. Add the onion and sauté till light golden. Add the ginger paste, garlic paste, turmeric powder, remaining chilli powder and salt. Sauté for one minute and add the potatoes. Mix well, remove from heat and set aside to cool. Pound the fried gram flour balls coarsely. Add to the potato mixture along with the coriander leaves, mint leaves, green chillies and lemon juice. Shape the mixture into balls.

•   Mix together three tablespoons of gram flour, three tablespoons of cornflour, the baking powder and some water to make a moderately thin batter. Heat the oil in a kadai; dip the potato balls in the batter and deep-fry, a few at a time, till golden. Drain on absorbent paper. Serve hot with Green Chutney (page 102)

BOOTE KE SAMOSE

Crispy samosas with a spicy green gram filling. This elegant savoury will enhance your collection of snack recipes.

Ingredients

4 tablespoons whole green gram
  (sabut moong), soaked
2½ cups refined flour (maida)
3 tablespoons oil + for deep-frying

1½ tablespoons green chilli paste
salt to taste
1 tablespoon lemon juice

Method

• Add two tablespoons of oil and half a cup of water to the refined flour and knead to make a moderately firm dough. Cover with a damp cloth and set aside for thirty minutes.

• Heat one tablespoon of oil in a pan; add the green chilli paste and sauté for two minutes. Add the green gram, salt and half a cup or just enough water to cook the gram. Cover and cook till dry. Sauté the mixture for three or four minutes. Stir in the lemon juice.

• Divide the dough into four equal portions and roll each portion out into an elongated puri. Cut each puri in half and shape each half into a cone. Stuff the cones with the green gram mixture and seal the edges with a little water.

• Heat the oil in a kadai and deep-fry the samosas till crisp and golden. Drain on absorbent paper. Serve hot with Green Chutney (page 102)

CHIPPE KA GOSHT

'Chippa' is an earthenware cooking pot. This dry meat dish absorbs the subtle flavour of the earth as it cooks.

Ingredients

600 grams boneless mutton, cut into
  2-inch pieces
salt to taste
1 teaspoon turmeric powder
3 teaspoons red chilli powder
2 tablespoons ginger paste

2 tablespoons garlic paste
2 tablespoons unripe green papaya paste
3 tablespoons oil
3 tablespoons lemon juice
2 tablespoons chopped fresh coriander
  leaves

Method

• Flatten the mutton pieces with a steak hammer to make quarter-inch thick round slices. Marinate the mutton in a mixture of salt, turmeric powder, chilli powder, ginger paste, garlic paste and green papaya paste for three hours, preferably in a refrigerator.

• Heat the oil in an earthenware pot (matka). Add the marinated mutton and stir-fry for about fifteen minutes over a low heat. Add three cups of water, cover and cook over a medium heat till tender. Increase the heat and cook, uncovered, till dry. Stir in the lemon juice and coriander leaves. Remove from heat and serve with naan.

DUM KE KABAB

It was Ustad Habib Pasha who taught me the finer nuances of making these melt-in-the-mouth kababs. The yogurt and cream mixed into the finely ground keema make the kababs moist and succulent.

Ingredients

450 grams minced mutton (keema)
½ tablespoon unripe green papaya paste
oil for deep-frying
2 medium onions, sliced
1 inch cinnamon
4 green cardamoms
3 cloves
½ teaspoon allspice (kabab chini)
1 teaspoon chironji (charoli)
½ teaspoon poppy seeds (khus khus)
1 tablespoon grated dried coconut
  (khopra)
3 dried red chillies, broken into pieces
½ teaspoon caraway seeds (shahi jeera)
3 green chillies
2 tablespoons chopped fresh coriander
  leaves

3-4 garlic cloves
½ inch ginger
1½ teaspoons gram flour (besan)
¾ cup yogurt, whisked
¼ cup cream
1 tablespoon lemon juice
salt to taste
a pinch of red chilli powder
a pinch of Garam Masala Powder (page 104)
1½ tablespoons pure ghee

Garnish

1 medium onion, cut into rings
a few fresh mint sprigs
1 lemon, cut into wedges

Method

•   Mix the green papaya paste into the keema and leave to marinate for fifteen minutes. Grind till smooth. Heat the oil in a kadai and deep-fry the onions till golden. Drain on absorbent paper.

•   Dry-roast the cinnamon, cardamoms, cloves and kabab chini separately till fragrant. Cool and grind to a fine powder. Dry-roast the chironji, poppy seeds, dried coconut, red chillies and caraway seeds separately till fragrant. Grind the spices together with the green chillies, coriander leaves, garlic and ginger to a smooth paste. Roast the gram flour over a low heat till fragrant.

•   Mix all the above ingredients with the keema and grind twice. Add half a cup of yogurt, the cream, lemon juice and salt. Cover and place in a refrigerator for thirty minutes.

•   Preheat the oven to 225°C/ 425°F/ Gas Mark 7.

•   Divide the chilled mixture into twenty-four equal portions and shape into balls. Grease your palms with a little oil and shape the balls into sausage shapes. Arrange on a greased tray and set aside.

•   Place the remaining yogurt in a small bowl; add a pinch each of chilli powder and garam masala powder and whisk thoroughly. Spoon a little of this mixture onto each kabab. Cook in the oven for twenty minutes, basting now and then with ghee. Remove from the oven and serve hot with onion rings, mint sprigs and lemon wedges.

GARELU

Twice-fried crisp doughnut-shaped dal wadas. The pepper and onion add new dimensions.

Ingredients

1 cup split black gram (dhuli urad dal), soaked
salt to taste
3 green chillies, chopped
4 baby onions, chopped

5-6 black peppercorns, roasted and coarsely crushed
½ teaspoon roasted cumin seeds
1 tablespoon chopped fresh coriander leaves
oil for deep-frying

Method

•   Drain and grind the urad dal to a coarse paste. Mix together the ground paste, salt, green chillies, onions, peppercorns, cumin seeds and coriander leaves.

•   Heat the oil in a kadai. Spoon a tablespoon of the dal mixture onto a sheet of plastic or a banana leaf. Hollow out the centre of the mixture to form a ring and gently slide into the oil. Deep-fry over a low heat till half-cooked. Drain on absorbent paper. Repeat the process with the rest of the mixture.

•   Increase the heat and re-fry all the garelu till golden brown. Drain and serve hot with Coconut Chutney (page 102).

LUKHMI

Lukhmis stuffed with keema are traditional Hyderabadi starters served at many a wedding banquet. The name is derived from 'luqma' which means crumb. The dough for the outer covering is kneaded with yogurt to make it meltingly soft.

Ingredients

250 grams minced mutton (keema)
125 grams refined flour (maida) + for
   dusting
salt to taste
a pinch of turmeric powder
½ teaspoon red chilli powder
½ teaspoon ginger paste

½ teaspoon garlic paste
1½ tablespoons oil + for deep-frying
2 tablespoons chopped fresh coriander leaves
2-3 green chillies, chopped
1 tablespoon lemon juice
2 tablespoons pure ghee
1 tablespoon yogurt

Method

• Place the keema with the salt, turmeric powder, chilli powder, ginger paste and garlic paste in a pan. Add half a cup of water and cook for fifteen to twenty minutes, or till the keema is tender.

• Heat one and a half tablespoons of oil in a pan; add the coriander leaves and green chillies and sauté for one minute. Add the keema and sauté till all the water has evaporated and the keema is dry. Stir in the lemon juice, remove from heat and set aside to cool.

• Add a little salt, the ghee, yogurt and one tablespoon of water to the refined flour in a bowl and knead into a soft dough. Cover the dough with cling film and refrigerate for half an hour.

• Divide the chilled dough into sixteen equal portions. Shape each portion into a ball, dust with maida and roll out into a five-inch long rectangle. Place a tablespoon of keema mixture in the centre, moisten the edges and fold the dough from the top down to cover the keema, sealing the edges on all three sides. Fold in one-third to the centre and bring over the remaining one-third over to make a book fold.

• Heat the oil in a kadai and deep-fry the lukhmi till golden. Drain on absorbent paper and serve hot.

MAKAI, BADAM AUR AKHROT KI TIKKI

Does the list of ingredients in this recipe seem long? Marvel at it because the intermingling of all the flavours and textures gives this tikki a uniqueness which is unsurpassed.

Ingredients

1½ cups (300 grams) corn kernels (makai), boiled and ground
20 almonds (badam), blanched, peeled and ground
16 walnut (akhrot) halves, chopped
200 grams lotus roots (bhein)
2 tablespoons oil + for shallow-frying
1 teaspoon caraway seeds (shahi jeera)
1 teaspoon red chilli powder
1 teaspoon black pepper powder
1 teaspoon fennel (saunf) powder

1 teaspoon Garam Masala Powder (page 104)
1 teaspoon chaat masala
100 grams cottage cheese (paneer), grated
salt to taste
½ cup grated processed cheese
1 tablespoon lemon juice
1 inch ginger, chopped
2 tablespoons chopped fresh coriander leaves
24 raisins (kishmish), chopped

Method

• Clean and scrape the lotus roots. Grate and boil until soft. Drain, squeeze out excess water and grind to a paste.

• Heat two tablespoons of oil in a kadai; add the caraway seeds and sauté till fragrant. Add the corn paste, almond paste and lotus root paste and sauté till the moisture evaporates and the mixture is dry. Add the chilli powder, pepper powder, fennel powder, garam masala powder and chaat masala and mix well.

• Add the paneer and salt and stir to mix. Cook till the mixture thickens and the oil separates. Remove from heat and stir in the processed cheese, lemon juice, ginger and coriander leaves. Set aside to cool.

• Divide the cooled mixture into twenty equal balls. Stuff the balls with walnuts and raisins and shape into tikkis. Heat a little oil in a frying pan and shallow-fry the tikkis on both sides. Drain on absorbent paper. Serve hot with Green Chutney (page 102)

MURTABAK

This is a Persian delicacy that has acquired many avatars during its journey from Persia down to Indonesia. The Hyderabadi version baked in layers is unique. It was Begum Mumtaz Khan who taught me how to cook it just right.

Ingredients

Chapatti
100 grams refined flour (maida) + for
   dusting
1 tablespoon oil
salt to taste

Filling
250 grams minced chicken (keema)
6 eggs
a few saffron threads
2 tablespoons oil
2 medium onions, chopped
1 teaspoon ginger paste

1 teaspoon garlic paste
1 teaspoon red chilli powder
½ teaspoon turmeric powder
salt to taste
1 teaspoon Garam Masala Powder (page 104)
2 teaspoons lemon juice
½ cup pure ghee
½ cup milk
150 grams processed cheese, grated
2 tablespoons chopped fresh coriander
   leaves
2 tablespoons chopped fresh mint leaves
10 green chillies, chopped

Method

•   Boil four eggs in hot water for twelve minutes. Drain and plunge in cold water. Peel and chop into small pieces. Beat the remaining two eggs in a bowl and set aside. Soak the saffron in two tablespoons of warm water.

•   For the chapattis, mix the refined flour with oil and salt. Rub the mixture between your fingertips till it resembles breadcrumbs. Add some water and knead into a soft dough. Cover with a damp cloth and set aside for half an hour. Divide the dough into nine equal portions. Dust a smooth surface with flour and roll out the dough into thin chapattis. Heat a tawa and cook the chapattis on both sides till done. Set aside.

•   For the filling, heat the oil in a kadai; add the onions and sauté till lightly browned. Add the ginger paste and garlic paste and sauté till the raw flavours disappear. Add the chilli powder and turmeric powder and sauté for three or four minutes. Add the chicken mince and salt and cook, stirring continuously, till the moisture dries up. Stir in the garam masala and lemon juice and remove from heat. Grind the mince in a blender to a coarse paste.

•   Preheat the oven to 180°C/ 350°F/ Gas Mark 4.

•   Brush a cake tin with a little ghee and cover the base with a thin chapatti. Sprinkle a little milk over the chapatti, followed by two tablespoons of mince, some chopped boiled egg, cheese, coriander leaves, mint leaves and green chillies. Brush with beaten egg. Cover with another chapatti and repeat the process once more ending with a chapatti. Make two more stacks and brush each one with saffron.

•   Cook in the oven for half an hour, or till golden brown and set. Turn out onto a plate and cut into wedges. Serve hot.

PATTHER KABAB

These kababs get their name from the hot stone slab on which they are grilled. The heated stone releases minerals that mix with the juices of the marinated pasandey and impart an extraordinary flavour.

Ingredients

800 grams boneless mutton, cut into
   1½-inch pieces
2 inches ginger
10 garlic cloves
5 green chillies
3-inch piece of unripe green papaya
4 tablespoons oil + for deep-frying
2 medium onions, sliced
2 tablespoons yogurt

1 teaspoon black pepper powder
1 teaspoon green cardamom powder
1 teaspoon Garam Masala Powder (page 104)
1 teaspoon lichen/stone flower (patther phool)
   powder
1 tablespoon malt vinegar
salt to taste
oil or ghee for basting

Method

• Pound the mutton with a steak hammer or the blunt side of a knife to make quarter-inch thick pasandey. Grind the ginger, garlic, green chillies and papaya to a fine paste.

• Heat the oil in a kadai and deep-fry the onions till brown. Drain, cool and grind with the yogurt to a fine paste. Mix together the ground spice paste, onion-yogurt paste, pepper powder, cardamom powder, garam masala powder, lichen powder, malt vinegar, salt and four tablespoons of oil. Coat the mutton pasandey well with the mixture and leave to marinate for three or four hours, preferably in a refrigerator.

• Take a flat slab of rough granite or kadappa stone that is about one and a half feet long, one foot wide and two inches thick. Wash the stone and place it firmly on two piles of bricks. Light a charcoal fire underneath the stone slab and heat it well. Season the stone by smearing it with oil when it is very hot. Sprinkle the stone with a little salt and wipe with a clean cloth. It is now ready to use.

• Sprinkle a little oil or ghee on the surface and place the marinated pasandey on the hot stone. Turn the pasandey a few times, basting occasionally with oil. Remove when cooked through,. Alternatively, the kababs can be cooked on a non-stick tawa over a gas flame. Serve with hot tandoori rotis and kachumber.

PHAL-SUBZ SEEKH

The humble banana, dressed up with mushrooms and broccoli, makes this tandoori starter fit for a royal repast.

Ingredients

2 unripe bananas, boiled, peeled and grated
2 medium potatoes, boiled and mashed
200 grams fresh button mushrooms, chopped
1 small carrot, grated
4 broccoli florets, chopped
1½ tablespoons butter
¾ teaspoon carom seeds (ajwain)
¾ tablespoon chopped fresh coriander leaves
¾ inch ginger, chopped
1½ fresh red chillies, chopped
salt to taste
12 prunes, chopped
½ teaspoon black salt
¾ teaspoon black pepper powder
½ teaspoon green cardamom powder
a pinch of sandalwood powder
a pinch of dried rose petal powder
½ cup breadcrumbs
1½ tablespoons oil

Method

• Heat the butter in a pan; add the carom seeds and sauté over medium heat for ten seconds. Add the mushrooms, carrot and broccoli and sauté till the moisture evaporates. Add the coriander leaves, ginger, red chillies and salt. Stir and remove from heat and set aside to cool.

• Place the cooled mixture in a blender with the grated bananas, mashed potatoes, prunes, black salt, pepper powder, cardamom powder, sandalwood powder, rose petal powder, and breadcrumbs and process till smooth. Divide the mixture into equal portions. Pat the mixture onto skewers into four-inch long seekh kababs.

• Preheat a tandoor. Cook the kababs in the tandoor for six or seven minutes, basting occasionally with oil. Alternatively, shape each portion into a croquette, arrange on a greased baking tray and grill in a preheated oven at 180°C/350°F/Gas Mark 4 for six or seven minutes. Arrange the kababs on a platter and serve hot with kachumber.

SHIKHAMPURI KABAB

A gourmet's delight: delicious yogurt enclosed in succulent mutton kababs will please the palate of the shikam (epicure).

Ingredients

2 cups minced mutton (keema)
½ cup split Bengal gram (chana dal),
 soaked
3-4 Kashmiri chillies, broken into bits
1 inch cinnamon
3-4 cloves
5-6 black peppercorns
1 tablespoon cumin seeds
1 tablespoon coriander seeds
2 green chillies, chopped
1 inch ginger, chopped
4-5 garlic cloves, chopped
salt to taste
1 teaspoon Garam Masala Powder
 (page 104)
1 tablespoon lemon juice

1 tablespoon sesame seeds (til)
oil for shallow-frying
2 eggs, beaten

Stuffing
½ cup drained (hung) yogurt
1 green chilli, chopped
1 large onion, chopped
2 tablespoons chopped fresh mint leaves
salt to taste
½ teaspoon roasted cumin seeds

To Serve
1 medium onion, cut into rings
½ cup Green Chutney (page 102)

Method

•   Dry-roast the chillies, cinnamon, cloves, peppercorns, cumin seeds and coriander seeds. Cool and grind to a fine powder.

•   In a large pan, combine the keema, chana dal, green chillies, ginger, garlic and salt to taste. Add two cups of water and bring to a boil. Lower the heat, add the powdered masala and simmer till almost done and the mixture is dry. Remove from heat and set aside to cool. Grind the cooled mixture to a smooth paste. Add the garam masala powder, lemon juice and sesame seeds and mix well. Divide the mixture into sixteen portions.

•   For the stuffing, mix the yogurt with the green chilli, onion, mint leaves, salt and roasted cumin seeds. Divide into sixteen equal portions. Flatten each portion of the mince mixture in the palm of your hand and place a portion of yogurt stuffing in the centre. Gather the edges, shape into a ball and flatten slightly.

•   Heat a little oil in a pan. Dip each kabab in the beaten egg and shallow-fry till golden brown. Drain on absorbent paper and serve hot with onion rings and green chutney.

TOOTAK

This baked delicacy has a rich semolina dough encasing a delicious paneer and potato filling. A Hindu contribution to the multifaceted Hyderabadi cuisine.

Ingredients

1 cup semolina (sooji/rawa)
salt to taste
½ cup pure ghee
½ cup grated khoya/mawa
½ cup milk
a few saffron threads
1 tablespoon rose water
1 tablespoon oil
1 teaspoon cumin seeds
1 inch ginger, chopped
1 teaspoon red chilli powder
1 teaspoon black pepper powder

2 teaspoons coriander powder
¼ teaspoon Garam Masala Powder
  (page 104)
200 grams cottage cheese (paneer),
  grated
1 potato, boiled and mashed
20 cashew nuts, chopped
15 raisins (kishmish)
1 tablespoon chopped fresh coriander
  leaves
1 tablespoon lemon juice

Method

• Mix together the semolina, salt, ghee, khoya and milk and knead into a soft dough. Cover with a damp cloth and rest the dough for two or three hours. Knead the dough once again and rest it for half an hour. Soak the saffron in the rose water.

• Heat the oil in a pan and add the cumin seeds. When they begin to change colour, add the ginger and sauté till light brown. Add the chilli powder, pepper powder, coriander powder, salt and garam masala powder. Cook for two or three minutes.

• Add the paneer, potato, cashew nuts and raisins; mix well and cook till completely dry. Stir in the coriander leaves and lemon juice. Divide the mixture into sixteen equal portions and set aside to cool.

• Preheat the oven to 200°C/400°F/Gas Mark 6.

• Divide the dough into sixteen equal portions. Shape each portion into a katori with your fingers; fill with one portion of the paneer-potato mixture, gather the edges together and roll into a ball. to enclose the filling. Flatten slightly and shape into an oval tootak. Arrange the tootaks on a baking tray and set aside for ten minutes. Brush the tootaks with saffron-rose water and cook in the oven for ten minutes. Serve hot.

ARBI FRY

Twice-fried crisp arbi tossed in masala and tamarind pulp: a perfect companion to a dal and parantha meal.

Ingredients

500 grams colocasia tubers (arbi)
1 tablespoon oil + for deep-frying
½ teaspoon cumin seeds
12 curry leaves
4 green chillies, slit
½ teaspoon coriander powder
a pinch of turmeric powder

½ teaspoon red chilli powder
½ teaspoon Garam Masala Powder
 (page 104)
salt to taste
4 teaspoons Tamarind Pulp (page 104)
2 tablespoons chopped fresh coriander leaves

Method

•   Wash and parboil the arbi in hot water till tender. Drain, cool and peel. Heat the oil in a kadai and deep-fry the arbi till pale gold. Drain on absorbent paper. Cool and press between your palms or cling film to flatten. Heat the oil again and deep-fry the arbi over high heat till golden. Drain on absorbent paper.

•   Heat one tablespoon of oil in a pan; add the cumin seeds, curry leaves and green chillies and sauté for thirty seconds. Add the coriander powder, turmeric powder, chilli powder, garam masala powder, salt and the fried arbi and stir-fry for three or four minutes. Add the tamarind pulp and stir-fry for another two minutes. Sprinkle coriander leaves and remove from heat. Serve hot.

PYAAZ KI TARKARI

Onions dominate this simple dish cooked with tamarind and red chillies. Traditionally it is very spicy but you can vary the chilli quotient to taste.

Ingredients

8 large onions, sliced
4 tablespoons oil
1 teaspoon ginger paste
1 teaspoon garlic paste

salt to taste
½ teaspoon turmeric powder
1 teaspoon red chilli powder
1 tablespoon Tamarind Pulp (page 104)

Method

•   Heat the oil in a pan; add the onions and sauté till light golden brown. Add the ginger and garlic pastes and sauté till the raw flavours disappear. Add the salt, turmeric powder and chilli powder and continue to sauté for two minutes. Sprinkle a little water and mix well. Lower the heat, cover and simmer for four or five minutes.

•   Add the tamarind pulp and cook over a medium heat for two or three minutes, or till the oil separates. Serve hot.

BAGHARE BAINGAN

Another famous Hyderabadi cross-cultural vegetarian dish: it has the classic touch of the North combining beautifully with Southern spice.

Ingredients

250 grams small brinjals (baingan)
2 medium onions, quartered
1½ teaspoons coriander seeds
1½ tablespoons sesame seeds (til)
2 tablespoons peanuts
½ teaspoon cumin seeds
¾ teaspoon poppy seeds (khus khus)
1 tablespoon grated dried coconut
   (khopra)
a pinch of fenugreek seeds (methi dana)

1 inch ginger, chopped
6-8 garlic cloves, chopped
salt to taste
a pinch of turmeric power
½ teaspoon red chilli powder
½ teaspoon grated jaggery (gur) or sugar
2 tablespoons Tamarind Pulp (page 104)
½ cup oil
a sprig of curry leaves

Method

•   Wash the brinjals and slit lengthways into four, with the quarters held together at the stalk end.

•   Dry-roast the onions on a tawa till soft and pale gold. Dry-roast the coriander seeds, sesame seeds, peanuts, cumin seeds, poppy seeds, dried coconut and fenugreek seeds all together till fragrant and they begin to change colour.

•   Grind together the roasted onions, roasted spices, ginger, garlic, salt, turmeric powder, chilli powder and jaggery to a very fine paste. Add the tamarind pulp and mix well. Stuff the slit brinjals with some masala and reserve the rest.

•   Heat the oil in a kadai; add the curry leaves and sauté for one minute. Add the stuffed brinjals and sauté for about ten minutes. Add the reserved masala and mix gently. Add two cups of water, cover and cook over low heat till the brinjals are completely cooked and the oil rises to the surface. Serve hot.

BHARE BAGHARE TAMATAR

When it comes to embellishing something as simple as a ripe tomato, this recipe will win hands down! With its rich cheesy stuffing and the peanut-flavoured gravy, it is worth the effort it takes.

Ingredients

8 medium firm red tomatoes
1½ tablespoons unsalted butter
5-6 medium fresh button mushrooms, chopped
½ cup grated cottage cheese (paneer)
3 tablespoons grated processed cheese
½ medium red capsicum, seeded and chopped
2 teaspoons chopped fresh coriander leaves
2 green chillies, chopped
12 cashew nuts, halved
salt to taste
¾ cup raw shelled peanuts

1 tablespoon oil + for deep-frying
2 medium onions, sliced
¼ teaspoon mustard seeds
¼ teaspoon cumin seeds
½ teaspoon caraway seeds (shahi jeera)
8 curry leaves
1½ tablespoons ginger paste
1 tablespoon garlic paste
¼ cup Tamarind Pulp (page 104)
1 teaspoon red chilli powder
½ teaspoon turmeric powder
2 teaspoons coriander powder
½ teaspoon roasted cumin powder

Method

• Blanch the tomatoes in boiling salted water for half a minute. Drain and peel. Slice off the top of each tomato and scoop out the seeds to make cups. Heat the butter in a pan and sauté the mushrooms until all the moisture evaporates. Remove and cool.

• Mix together the mushrooms, paneer, cheese, capsicum, coriander leaves, green chillies, cashew nuts and salt. Spoon the mixture into the tomato cups and set aside.

• Roast the peanuts, cool and grind with a little water into a fine paste. Heat the oil in a kadai and deep-fry the onions till golden brown. Drain on absorbent paper.

• Heat one tablespoon of oil in a separate kadai; add the mustard seeds, cumin seeds and caraway seeds and sauté till they begin to splutter. Add the curry leaves and sauté for half a minute. Add the ginger paste and garlic paste and sauté until lightly browned. Stir in the tamarind pulp and sauté for three or four minutes over medium heat.

• Add the fried onions, chilli powder, turmeric powder, coriander powder and cumin powder and continue to sauté till the oil rises to the surface. Add the peanut paste and sauté until the mixture thickens. Add three cups of water and salt and bring to a boil. Lower heat; carefully add the stuffed tomatoes to the simmering gravy, and cook for four or five minutes. Do not overcook the tomatoes; they should be firm and hold their shape. Serve hot.

DIWANI HANDI

This delicacy used to be cooked for royalty. Handi is a uniquely shaped vessel made of brass, copper or aluminium.

Ingredients

3 medium potatoes, peeled and cut into
    ½-inch cubes
3 medium carrots, cut into ½-inch cubes
10-12 French beans, cut diagonally
10-12 broad beans (sem ki phalli), cut
    diagonally
4-6 small brinjals, slit
½ cup green peas
3 tablespoons oil
2 medium onions, sliced
2-3 green chillies, seeded and chopped
1 tablespoon ginger paste

1 tablespoon garlic paste
1 teaspoon red chilli powder
½ teaspoon turmeric powder
salt to taste
2 tablespoons yogurt
½ bunch (150 grams) fresh fenugreek leaves
    (methi), chopped
2 tablespoons chopped fresh coriander
    leaves
½ teaspoon Garam Masala Powder
    (page 104)

Method

• Heat the oil in a handi; add the onions and sauté till light brown. Add the green chillies, ginger paste and garlic paste and sauté for one minute. Add the chilli powder, turmeric powder and salt and mix. Add the yogurt and sauté for two or three minutes.

• Add all the vegetables and simmer, covered, till tender. Add the fenugreek leaves, coriander leaves and garam masala powder; stir and cook for three or four minutes.

• Serve hot with Indian bread.

DOODHI PANEER KA SUKHA SALAN

An interesting combination of bottle gourd and cottage cheese with multi-coloured capsicums. The coconut masala makes it rather special.

Ingredients

600 grams bottle gourd (doodhi/lauki), cut into ¾-inch diamonds
200 grams cottage cheese (paneer), cut into ¾-inch diamonds
1 medium red capsicum, cut into ¾-inch diamonds
1 medium yellow capsicum, cut into ¾-inch diamonds
1 medium green capsicum, cut into ¾-inch diamonds
2 tablespoons grated dried coconut (khopra)
1 tablespoon peanuts
1 teaspoon sesame seeds (til)
1 lemon-sized ball tamarind
4 tablespoons oil + for deep-frying
1 medium onion, sliced

¼ teaspoon cumin seeds
¼ teaspoon fenugreek seeds (methi dana)
¼ teaspoon fennel seeds (saunf)
¼ teaspoon onion seeds (kalonji)
¼ teaspoon mustard seeds
8 curry leaves
2 teaspoons ginger-garlic paste
4 green chillies, chopped
1 teaspoon coriander powder
½ teaspoon roasted cumin powder
¼ teaspoon turmeric powder
½ teaspoon red chilli powder
salt to taste
½ teaspoon Garam Masala Powder (page 104)
1 tablespoon chopped fresh coriander leaves

Method

• Dry-roast the coconut, peanuts and sesame seeds. Cool and grind to a fine paste. Soak the tamarind for thirty minutes in warm water, squeeze out and strain the pulp.

• Heat the oil in a kadai; deep-fry the onion till golden brown. Drain on absorbent paper.

• Heat four tablespoons of oil in a pan. Add the cumin seeds, fenugreek seeds, fennel seeds, onion seeds and mustard seeds. When they begin to splutter, add the curry leaves, and ginger-garlic paste. Sauté till the raw flavours disappear. Add the green chillies and doodhi and sauté for four or five minutes. Add all capsicums and cook, covered, for ten to fifteen minutes.

• Add the coriander powder, cumin powder, turmeric powder and chilli powder. Sauté for three or four minutes. Add the fried onions and salt. Stir-fry for three or four minutes. Add the peanut paste and stir-fry till the oil separates. Stir in the tamarind pulp. Add the paneer and toss well to coat with the spices. Sprinkle garam masala and coriander leaves. Stir and remove from heat. Serve hot with Indian bread.

KACHCHE KELE KE KOFTE

An excellent way of turning bananas into something special. Goes best with paranthas.

Ingredients

Kofte
4 medium-sized unripe bananas
1 inch ginger, chopped
4 green chillies, chopped
2 tablespoons chopped fresh coriander
  leaves
½ teaspoon Garam Masala Powder
  (page 104)
1 tablespoon lemon juice
4 tablespoons cornflour
salt to taste
oil for deep-frying

Stuffing
7-8 cashew nuts, roasted and chopped
4 dried figs (anjeer), chopped
6 raisins (kishmish), lightly roasted
½ inch ginger, chopped
a few sprigs of fresh mint leaves, roughly
  torn
½ teaspoon chaat masala
1 tablespoon lemon juice

Gravy
½ cup cashew nuts, soaked
¼ cup melon seeds (charmagaz), soaked
¼ cup oil
6 green cardamoms
2 black cardamoms
4 cloves
2 one-inch sticks cinnamon
2 medium onions, sliced
1 tablespoon ginger-garlic paste
4 medium tomatoes, puréed
1 teaspoon red chilli powder
2 teaspoons coriander powder
½ teaspoon turmeric powder
½ teaspoon Garam Masala Powder (page 104)
2 one-inch pieces of ginger, cut into thin
  strips
2 tablespoons chopped fresh coriander
  leaves
2 teaspoons cream (malai)

Method

•	For the kofte, boil the bananas with the skins on until soft. Peel and mash till smooth. Add the ginger, green chillies and coriander leaves and mix. Add the garam masala powder, lemon juice, two tablespoons of cornflour and salt. Mix thoroughly. Divide the mixture into sixteen equal portions. Shape each portion into a ball and set aside.

•	For the stuffing, mix together the cashew nuts, figs, raisins and ginger. Add the mint leaves, chaat masala and lemon juice. Divide into sixteen equal portions. Stuff a portion of the cashew nut mixture into each banana portion, roll in the remaining cornflour, arrange on a platter and refrigerate for half an hour.

•	Heat the oil in a kadai and deep-fry the kofte till light brown in colour. Drain on absorbent paper and set aside.

•	For the gravy, grind the soaked cashew nuts and melon seeds to a fine paste with a little water. Heat one-fourth cup of oil in a pan. Add the green and black cardamoms, the cloves and cinnamon and stir-fry till the cardamoms change colour. Add the onions and fry till golden brown. Add the ginger-garlic paste and sauté for three or four minutes. Add the tomato purée, chilli powder, coriander powder and turmeric powder and stir-fry till the oil separates.

•	Add the cashew nut-melon seed paste and cook until the gravy thickens. Add approximately two cups of water and cook over a low heat for about ten minutes or until the gravy thickens. Sprinkle the garam masala and remove from heat.

•	Arrange the kofte in a serving dish and pour the gravy over. Garnish with ginger strips, coriander leaves and cream and serve hot.

KAJU KHUMB MAKHANA

Ideal for those who love richly-textured vegetarian dishes. The cashew nuts add a chewy bite to the softness of mushrooms and lotus seeds. Simply superb!

Ingredients

1 cup whole cashew nuts (kaju), soaked
500 grams fresh button mushrooms
(khumb)
2 cups puffed lotus seeds (makhane)
oil for shallow-frying
½ cup yogurt
1 tablespoon coriander powder
1½ teaspoons red chilli powder
1 teaspoon turmeric powder
2 tablespoons pure ghee
1 teaspoon cumin seeds

3 medium onions, chopped
2 teaspoons ginger paste
2 teaspoons garlic paste
2 teaspoons black pepper powder
1½ cups fresh tomato purée
salt to taste
1 teaspoon Garam Masala Powder (page 104)
1 tablespoon honey (optional)
1 tablespoon lemon juice
2 tablespoons chopped fresh coriander
leaves

Method

• Remove the stalks of the mushrooms, clean and boil until three-fourth cooked. Drain and set aside. Heat the oil in a kadai and shallow-fry the makhane for half a minute. Drain and soak in a bowl of water.

• Place the yogurt in a bowl; add the coriander powder, chilli powder and turmeric powder and whisk well to mix.

• Heat the ghee in a pan; add the cumin seeds and when they begin to change colour, add the onions and sauté until translucent. Add the ginger paste and garlic paste and sauté for five minutes. Add the pepper powder and sauté for two minutes. Add the mushrooms and continue to sauté for five minutes. Add the yogurt mixture and cook till the oil separates.

• Add the tomato purée and salt and sauté till the oil separates again. Add two and a half cups of water and bring to a boil; lower heat and add the cashew nuts and makhane. Cover and simmer, stirring occasionally, for eight to ten minutes. Sprinkle the garam masala powder and mix. Stir in the honey and lemon juice. Garnish with coriander leaves and serve with Indian bread.

KARELE KA SALAN

Bitter gourd cooked with the traditional tilli (sesame seed) - phalli (peanut) Hyderabadi combination. You can be assured of encores!

Ingredients

350 grams bitter gourds (karela)
½ teaspoon turmeric powder
salt to taste
4 tablespoons oil
2 small onions, chopped
1 inch ginger, chopped
6 garlic cloves, chopped
1 tablespoon coriander seeds
¾ teaspoon cumin seeds

1½ tablespoons sesame seeds (til)
2 tablespoons peanuts
3 dried red chillies, broken into large bits
2 tablespoons Tamarind Pulp (page 104)
1½ teaspoons grated jaggery (gur)
¼ teaspoon Garam Masala Powder (page 104)
2 tablespoons chopped fresh coriander
  leaves

Method

•   Lightly scrape the skin off the karele. Slit lengthways and remove the seeds and pulp. Rub half the turmeric powder and salt into the karele and set aside for fifteen to twenty minutes. Wash under running water and drain well.

•   Heat one tablespoon of oil in a pan and lightly roast the onions, ginger, garlic, coriander seeds, cumin seeds, sesame seeds, peanuts and red chillies. Cool and grind to a fine paste.

•   Mix the paste with the tamarind pulp, remaining turmeric powder, the jaggery and garam masala powder. Stuff the karele with the masala and tie with a thread. Reserve the remaining masala.

•   Heat the remaining oil in a pan; place the karele in it one by one. Shallow-fry for five minutes, turning them from time to time to brown evenly on all sides. Add the remaining masala and half a cup of water, cover and cook till the karele are tender. Stir gently to coat with the masala. Remove from heat, garnish with coriander leaves and serve hot.

MIRCHI KA SALAN

It is probably the most popular of the Hyderabadi vegetarian dishes made with the famous tilli (sesame seed) - phalli (peanut) masala. It is generally served with Hyderabadi Biryani.

Ingredients

18-20 large green chillies
2 tablespoons oil + for deep-frying
2 tablespoons sesame seeds (til)
1 tablespoon coriander seeds
1 teaspoon cumin seeds
½ cup roasted peanuts
2 dried red chillies, broken into bits
1 inch ginger, chopped

6-8 garlic cloves
1 teaspoon mustard seeds
8-10 curry leaves
1 medium onion, grated
1 teaspoon turmeric powder
2 tablespoons Tamarind Pulp (page 104)
salt to taste

Method

• Wash, wipe and slit the green chillies lengthways without separating into two. Heat the oil in a kadai and deep-fry the chillies for one minute. Drain on absorbent paper and set aside.

• Dry-roast the sesame seeds, coriander seeds and cumin seeds. Cool and grind to a paste along with the peanuts, red chillies, ginger and garlic.

• Heat two tablespoons of oil in a pan and add the mustard seeds. When they begin to splutter add the curry leaves and sauté for half a minute. Add the onion and sauté, stirring continuously, till light golden brown.

• Add the turmeric powder and mix well. Add the masala paste and cook for three minutes, stirring continuously. Stir in one and a half cups of water and bring to a boil. Lower the heat and cook for ten minutes. Stir in the tamarind pulp (mix the pulp with half a cup of water, if it is too thick). Add the fried green chillies and salt and cook over a low heat for eight to ten minutes. Serve hot.

PANEER TAMATAR KA KHUT

Pieces of paneer cooked in a silky smooth tomato gravy, it has everything ranging from a fiery red colour to the unique Southern taste of curry leaves, dried red chillies and cumin seeds.

Ingredients

250 grams cottage cheese (paneer)
8-10 medium tomatoes, chopped
½ lemon-sized ball tamarind
2 one-inch pieces ginger, chopped
10-12 garlic cloves, crushed
6-8 dried red chillies, broken into large bits
1 tablespoon sesame oil
1 teaspoon mustard seeds
1 teaspoon cumin seeds

20 curry leaves
3 one-inch sticks cinnamon
1 teaspoon turmeric powder
2 teaspoons coriander powder
1 teaspoon roasted cumin powder
salt to taste
¼ cup roasted Bengal gram, powdered
¼ cup coconut milk

Method

•   Cut the paneer into fingers. Soak the tamarind in half a cup of warm water for half an hour; squeeze out the pulp, strain and set aside.

•   Heat half a cup of water in a pan; add the tomatoes, ginger, garlic and red chillies and bring to a boil. Lower the heat, cover and simmer for fifteen to twenty minutes, or till the gravy is reduced to half the original quantity. Remove from heat and set aside to cool. Pass the cooled mixture through a fine mesh or a soup strainer.

•   Heat the sesame oil in a pan; add the mustard seeds and cumin seeds and sauté until the mustard seeds begin to splutter. Add the curry leaves, cinnamon, turmeric powder, coriander powder and cumin powder and sauté for one minute.

•   Add the strained tomato mixture and bring to a boil. Stir in the tamarind pulp and salt. Add the roasted Bengal gram powder and mix thoroughly. Lower the heat and stir in the coconut milk and paneer. Simmer for two or three minutes and serve hot.

ASIF JAHI PASANDEY

Mir Qumaruddin, the first Nizam of Hyderabad, also known as Asif Jah, was a great foodie. And this was his favourite dish and therefore the name. This pasandey recipe will transport you to the era of slow cooking and mellow flavours.

Ingredients

600 grams boneless mutton, cut into 1-inch cubes
24 almonds, blanched
6 cloves
6 green cardamoms
2 inches cinnamon
2 teaspoons unripe green papaya paste
2 teaspoons garlic paste
1 teaspoon ginger paste
5-6 black peppercorns, coarsely ground
salt to taste
½ cup oil

1½ teaspoons red chilli powder
½ cup browned onion paste
¼ cup ground grated fresh coconut paste
½ cup yogurt, whisked
2 tablespoons chopped fresh coriander leaves
a few sprigs of fresh mint leaves
6 green chillies, slit
a few saffron threads, soaked in 1 tablespoon of warm milk
2 teaspoons kewra water

Method

• Place the mutton cubes on a work-top and flatten them with a steak hammer or the handle of a heavy knife, into quarter-inch thick pieces (pasandey). Peel and slice five almonds for garnishing, and grind the rest to a fine paste. Roast the cloves, cardamoms and cinnamon lightly and grind to a fine powder.

• In a bowl, mix together the mutton pasandey, papaya paste, garlic paste, ginger paste, ground peppercorns and salt. Marinate the pasandey for about forty-five minutes, preferably in the refrigerator.

• Heat the oil in a pan; add the marinated mutton and sear over high heat for two or three minutes. Lower heat, add the chilli powder and browned onion paste and continue to sauté, sprinkling water at regular intervals (to prevent the mutton from sticking to the pan), till the mutton is half-cooked.

• Add the almond paste, coconut paste, yogurt, coriander leaves and half the mint leaves, roughly torn. Sauté till the gravy clings to the mutton. Add two cups of water and bring to a boil. Add the slit green chillies, cover and cook for twenty to twenty-five minutes, or till the mutton is tender.

• Add the saffron-flavoured milk, kewra water and sprinkle with the roasted spice powder. Stir and remove from heat. Serve, garnished with sliced almonds and remaining mint leaves.

Chef's Tip : You can request the butcher to cut and flatten the mutton into pasandey.

CHANDI KORMA

A rich and silky smooth nutty gravy that coats the chicken, enhanced with a layer of silver varq. A regal sight indeed.

Ingredients

1 whole chicken (1 kilogram), cut into 12 pieces
silver varq, to garnish
3 tablespoons oil
3 medium onions, sliced
1 tablespoon ginger paste
1 tablespoon garlic paste
1 tablespoon green chilli paste
¼ cup almonds, ground

½ cup grated khoya/mawa
1 cup yogurt
1 teaspoon white pepper powder
4 tablespoons cream
½ teaspoon green cardamom powder
½ teaspoon rose petal powder
5-6 almonds, slivered
5-6 pistachios, slivered

Method

• Heat the oil in a pan; add the onions and sauté till golden brown. Stir in the ginger and garlic pastes. Add the green chilli paste and sauté for five minutes. Add the almond paste, khoya and yogurt. Cook over a low heat for fifteen to twenty minutes. Sprinkle the white pepper powder and mix well.

• Add the chicken and cook over a low heat for another ten minutes, stirring occasionally. Pour in one cup of water and simmer for another five minutes till the chicken is cooked. Stir in the cream.

• Add the cardamom powder and rose petal powder, simmer for two minutes and remove from heat. Garnish with silver varq, almond and pistachio slivers and serve hot.

Note: For a spicier version, increase the green chilli paste or white pepper powder.

DALCHA

Mutton cooked with a combination of dals, subtly soured, with tamarind with the typical Southern seasoning of curry leaves, cumin seeds and dried red chillies. An extremely popular Hyderabadi dish.

Ingredients

500 grams boneless mutton, cut into 1½-inch pieces
½ cup split Bengal gram (chana dal), soaked
$^1/_8$ cup split green gram (dhuli moong dal), soaked
¼ cup split red lentils (masoor dal), soaked
¾ teaspoon turmeric powder
salt to taste
2 tablespoons oil
4 green cardamoms
2 black cardamoms
6 cloves
2 one-inch sticks cinnamon
2 medium onions, sliced
1 teaspoon ginger paste

1 teaspoon garlic paste
1 teaspoon coriander powder
3 green chillies, chopped
6-8 roughly torn fresh mint leaves
2 tablespoons chopped fresh coriander leaves

Seasoning
2 tablespoons pure ghee
2 tablespoons Tamarind Pulp (page 104)
1 teaspoon cumin seeds
5 garlic cloves, chopped
8-10 curry leaves
½ tablespoon coriander powder
1 teaspoon roasted cumin powder

Method

• Drain and cook the chana dal, moong dal and masoor dal in two cups of water along with one-fourth teaspoon turmeric powder and salt until soft. (The dals should be completely mashed.)

• Heat the oil in a pan; add the green and black cardamoms, cloves and cinnamon and sauté till fragrant. Add the onions and sauté till golden. Add the ginger paste and garlic paste and sauté for two minutes. Add the mutton, increase the heat and sauté for two or three minutes.

• Lower the heat, add the coriander powder, remaining turmeric powder and green chillies and sauté for five minutes. Add salt to taste. Add two cups of water and bring the mixture to a boil. Lower the heat and simmer until the mutton is tender. Add the cooked dals and cook for five minutes until the dal is well incorporated into the gravy.

• For the seasoning, heat the ghee in a separate pan; add the tamarind pulp, cumin seeds, garlic, curry leaves, coriander powder and cumin powder and sauté over a medium heat for two minutes. Add the seasoning to the dalcha and cook, covered, for three or four minutes. Serve hot, garnished with mint and coriander leaves.

DUM KI MACHLI

Fish marinated in an exotic mix of yogurt, nuts, poppy seeds and khoya. The result is something memorable.

Ingredients

600 grams king fish (seer fish/surmai) fillets, cut into 2-inch cubes
2 teaspoons ginger-garlic paste
1 tablespoon lemon juice
salt to taste
3 cloves
2 one-inch sticks cinnamon
½ teaspoon caraway seeds (shahi jeera)
5 green cardamoms
12 cashew nuts
1 teaspoon chironji (charoli)
2 teaspoons poppy seeds (khus khus)
½ cup browned fried onions
1 cup yogurt
1 cup grated khoya/mawa
a few sprigs of fresh mint, roughly torn
2 tablespoons chopped fresh coriander leaves
2-3 green chillies, chopped
½ teaspoon turmeric powder
a few saffron threads, soaked in 1 tablespoon of water
1 teaspoon Garam Masala Powder (page 104)
¼ cup + 3 tablespoons oil
2 lemons, cut into wedges

Method

• Marinate the fish in a mixture of the ginger-garlic paste, lemon juice and salt for thirty minutes. Lightly roast the cloves, cinnamon, caraway seeds and cardamoms and grind to a fine powder.

• Dry-roast the cashew nuts, chironji and poppy seeds and grind to a fine paste. Grind the browned onions with one and a half tablespoons of yogurt to a fine paste. Whisk the remaining yogurt with the grated khoya till smooth.

• In a bowl, mix together the cashew nut paste, browned onion paste, freshly ground masala powder and yogurt-khoya mixture. Add the fresh mint and coriander leaves and the green chillies. Add the turmeric powder, saffron and garam masala powder and whisk again. Add one-fourth cup of oil and whisk once more. Mix the marinade into the fish and set aside for fifteen minutes.

• Heat the remaining oil in a frying pan; place the fish with the marinade in the pan and shallow-fry for about seven to eight minutes, or till both sides are evenly browned.

• Serve hot, garnished with lemon wedges.

HALEEM

'Haleem' is an Arabic word meaning patience. It is aptly named as the dish requires many hours of slow cooking. It is usually eaten during Ramadan for Iftar (breaking the fast).

Ingredients

500 grams boneless mutton, cut into ½-inch cubes
½ cup broken wheat (dalia)
1 tablespoon split black gram (dhuli urad dal)
1 tablespoon split Bengal gram (chana dal)
1 tablespoon split green gram (dhuli moong dal)
1 cup yogurt
salt to taste
4 large onions, sliced and deep-fried till brown

1 tablespoon green chilli paste
1 tablespoon ginger-garlic paste
1 teaspoon caraway seeds (shahi jeera)
1 teaspoon black peppercorns
6 cups mutton stock
1 tablespoon chopped fresh mint leaves
1 teaspoon Garam Masala Powder (page 104)
¼ cup pure ghee
½ cup milk
a few sprigs of fresh mint
3-4 lemon wedges

Method

• Soak the broken wheat for three or four hours in two cups of water. Soak the urad dal, chana dal and moong dal together in one cup of water. Marinate the mutton in the yogurt and salt for one hour, preferably in a refrigerator.

• Place the soaked dalia and dals in a pressure cooker. Add the marinated mutton, green chilli paste, ginger-garlic paste, shahi jeera, peppercorns and mutton stock and mix well. Add salt to taste, the mint, garam masala powder and half the fried onions. Cover the cooker with the lid and cook under pressure till the pressure is released six times (six whistles).

• Remove the lid when the pressure has completely reduced. Remove the mutton pieces with a slotted spoon and set aside. Process the remaining mixture till smooth. Add the mutton back into the mixture.

• Heat the ghee in a pan; pour the haleem into the pan and bring to a boil. Lower the heat and simmer for ten minutes. Adjust the consistency by adding milk as required. Serve, garnished with the remaining fried onions, mint and lemon wedges.

HARA MASALA MURGH

Tender chicken cooked in a rich coriander gravy. Perfect with hot fluffy rotis.

Ingredients

1 whole chicken (1 kilogram), cut into 8 pieces
½ cup chopped fresh coriander leaves
4 tablespoons chopped fresh mint leaves
¼ coconut, grated
6 green chillies, seeded and chopped
3 tablespoons oil
4 large onions, chopped
10-12 curry leaves

1 tablespoon ginger paste
1 tablespoon garlic paste
1 tablespoon roasted cumin powder
1 tablespoon coriander powder
2 tablespoons almond paste
¾ cup yogurt
salt to taste
½ cup cream
1 teaspoon Garam Masala Powder (page 104)

Method

•   Grind together the coriander and mint leaves, coconut and green chillies to a smooth chutney.

•   Heat the oil in a deep pan; add the onions and sauté over a medium heat till golden brown. Add the curry leaves, ginger paste and garlic paste and sauté for three or four minutes, or till the raw flavours disappear. Add the cumin powder and coriander powder and continue to sauté for two minutes. Add the chicken and sauté for five minutes. Add the almond paste and sauté until the oil separates and the gravy is thick.

•   Add the yogurt and salt and cook for another three or four minutes. Add the green chutney and cook for two or three minutes. Stir in the cream and cook till the chicken is tender. Sprinkle garam masala powder, stir and remove from heat. Serve hot with rotis.

LAGAN KA KEEMA

A perfect dish to give your guests the royal treatment at a wedding! Minced meat with all the added flavours of spices and seeds is rounded off with a smoky flavour.

Ingredients

1 kilogram minced lamb (keema)
4 onions, sliced and deep-fried till golden
2 tablespoons poppy seeds (khus khus)
2 tablespoons chironji (charoli)
2 two-inch pieces dried coconut (khopra)
1 teaspoon allspice (kabab chini)
15 cloves
2 one-inch sticks cinnamon
8 green cardamoms
4 black cardamoms
a few saffron threads
2 tablespoons warm milk
8 tablespoons pure ghee
2 teaspoons caraway seeds (shahi jeera)

2 tablespoons ginger paste
2 tablespoons garlic paste
4 teaspoons coriander powder
2 teaspoons cumin powder
3 teaspoons red chilli powder
salt to taste
1 cup yogurt, whisked
4 tablespoons chopped fresh mint leaves +
    2 sprigs, to garnish
4 tablespoons chopped fresh coriander
    leaves
4 tablespoons lemon juice
1 lemon, cut into wedges
a few pieces of charcoal

Method

• Grind half the fried onions and reserve the rest for garnishing.

• Dry-roast the poppy seeds, chironji, and khopra till lightly browned. Cool and grind to a fine paste. Dry-roast the allspice, five cloves, the cinnamon and green and black cardamoms. Cool and grind to a fine powder. Soak the saffron in warm milk and set aside.

• Heat three tablespoons of ghee in a flat-bottomed pan. Add the caraway seeds, ginger paste and garlic paste and sauté for two or three minutes, or till the raw flavours disappear. Add the coriander powder, cumin powder and chilli powder and sauté for two or three minutes. Add the minced lamb and sauté over a low heat. Add the poppy seed paste, stir and cook for four or five minutes. Add salt and stir.

• Add the yogurt and simmer for another four or five minutes. Add the mint and coriander leaves, stir and cook for two minutes. Stir in the saffron-flavoured milk. Add the roasted spice powder and mix well. Stir in the lemon juice and remove from heat.

• Make a well in the centre of the mince and place an onion skin in it. Place a red-hot piece of charcoal on the onion skin. Pour the remaining ghee over the charcoal and place the remaining cloves on it. Cover the pan immediately and leave to stand for ten minutes so that the smoky flavours are absorbed by the mince. Remove the charcoal and discard.

• To serve, transfer the keema to a large serving dish and garnish with the reserved fried onions, sprigs of mint and lemon wedges.

KAIRI MURGH

This dish is ideal for hot summer days when unripe green mango acts as both a souring and cooling agent.

Ingredients

1 whole chicken (1 kilogram), cut into 2-inch
  pieces
2 medium-sized unripe green mangoes
1½ teaspoons ginger paste
1½ teaspoons garlic paste
salt to taste
2 teaspoons Garam Masala Powder (page 104)
1½ teaspoons green chilli paste ·
4-5 cloves

3 tablespoons oil
2 medium onions, sliced
¼ teaspoon turmeric powder
1½ teaspoons red chilli powder
2 teaspoons coriander powder
2 tablespoons chopped fresh coriander
  leaves
a few pieces of charcoal

Method

•   Peel and cut the green mangoes into small pieces. Purée half the mangoes.

•   In a bowl, marinate the chicken in a mixture of half the ginger paste, half the garlic paste, salt, half the garam masala powder, half the green chilli paste and the puréed mango for about an hour, preferably in the refrigerator.

•   Heat a piece of charcoal over an open flame till red-hot; place it in a katori (small stainless steel bowl) and place in the centre of the marinated chicken. Place the cloves on the coal and pour one tablespoon of oil over, immediately covering the bowl with a lid. Leave to stand for a few minutes so that the smoky flavours are absorbed by the chicken. Remove the charcoal and discard.

•   Heat the remaining oil in a kadai; add the onions and sauté till translucent. Add the remaining ginger paste, garlic paste and green chilli paste and sauté for two minutes. Add the marinated chicken, turmeric powder, chilli powder, coriander powder, remaining garam masala powder and chopped green mango. Stir to coat the chicken evenly with the masala.

•   Cook over a high heat for five or six minutes. Adjust salt, add the coriander leaves and three-fourth cup of water. Cover and cook for ten to twelve minutes, or till tender. Serve hot.

MURGH ZAFRANI DO PYAAZA

Chicken in an almond-rich gravy finished off with a generous pinch of saffron.

Ingredients

800 grams chicken on the bone, cut into
  1-inch pieces
a generous pinch of saffron
25 almonds, roasted
1 tablespoon chironji (charoli), roasted
1 tablespoon poppy seeds (khus khus),
  roasted
½ cup oil
2 medium onions, sliced

3 teaspoons ginger paste
1 teaspoon garlic paste
3 teaspoons red chilli powder
1 teaspoon turmeric powder
salt to taste
1 cup yogurt
3 cups chicken stock
½ teaspoon Garam Masala Powder (page 104)

Method

- Grind the almonds, chironji and poppy seeds together.

- Heat the oil in a pan and sauté the onions till golden. Add the ginger paste and garlic paste and sauté for two minutes. Stir in the chilli powder and turmeric powder. Add the chicken and sauté for five minutes. Sprinkle a little water from time to time so that the masala does not burn. Add salt.

- Add the yogurt and cook for another minute. Add the ground almond paste and cook for five minutes, stirring continuously. Add the chicken stock and bring the mixture to a boil. Lower the heat, cover and simmer for twenty minutes till the chicken is tender. Add the garam masala powder and saffron, stir and remove from heat. Serve with paranthas.

NALLI NIHARI

The word 'nihari' means fasting. This rich stew, slow-cooked overnight, is usually eaten at the sehri at the crack of dawn before the day's fast begins during the month of Ramadan.

Ingredients

500 grams lamb marrow bones (nalli)
2½ tablespoons Nihari Masala (page 104)
2 tablespoons pure ghee
2 medium onions, sliced and deep-fried till golden brown
½ inch ginger, cut into thin strips

2 tablespoons wholewheat flour (atta)
salt to taste
1 tablespoon lemon juice
2 tablespoons chopped fresh coriander leaves

Method

• Heat the ghee in a pressure cooker. Add the nalli and nihari masala and sauté for two minutes. Add four cups of water and cook under pressure till the pressure is released eight times (eight whistles). This may take about half an hour.

• Remove the lid when the pressure has completely reduced and transfer the contents to a kadai. Bring the mixture to a boil, stir in half the fried onions and half the ginger and simmer for two minutes.

• Combine the wholewheat flour with six tablespoons of water and mix well till smooth. Add to the nalli mixture and continue to simmer till the gravy thickens. Add salt and stir in the lemon juice. Serve, garnished with the remaining fried onions, remaining ginger and the chopped coriander leaves.

CHAR DAL KA DALCHA

Four dals and bottle gourd, flavoured with spices seasoned in pure ghee.

Ingredients

¼ cup split Bengal gram (chana dal)
2 tablespoons split lentils (masoor dal)
¼ cup split pigeon peas (arhar dal/ toovar dal)
2 tablespoons split green gram (dhuli moong dal)
1 teaspoon turmeric powder
1½ teaspoons red chilli powder
salt to taste
1 lemon-sized ball tamarind
3 tablespoons oil
2 medium onions, sliced

2 teaspoons ginger paste
5-6 green chillies, slit
400 grams bottle gourd (lauki), cut into 1-inch pieces

Seasoning
2 tablespoons pure ghee
1 teaspoon cumin seeds
5-6 dried red chillies, broken in half
12-15 curry leaves
6-8 garlic cloves, chopped

Method

• Soak all the dals in plenty of water for at least half an hour. Drain and place in a pressure cooker with half a teaspoon of turmeric powder, half a teaspoon of chilli powder, salt and four cups of water. Pressure-cook for four or five minutes, or till completely cooked.

• Soak the tamarind in one cup of warm water for half an hour. Squeeze out the pulp, strain and set aside.

• Heat the oil in a pan; add the onions and sauté till light brown. Add the remaining chilli and turmeric powders, the ginger paste and slit green chillies. Sauté for a few seconds and add the lauki. Sauté for three or four minutes and add the cooked dals. Cook, covered, over medium heat for about ten minutes, or till the lauki is tender.

• Add the tamarind pulp and half a cup of water and cook over medium heat for four or five minutes, stirring occasionally. Lower heat and simmer for another five minutes.

• For the seasoning, heat the ghee in a small pan; add the cumin seeds and when they begin to change colour, add the red chillies and curry leaves. Sauté for a few seconds, add the garlic and sauté till the garlic turns light brown. Pour the mixture into the dal, cover the pan with a lid immediately to trap the flavours. Serve hot.

KHATTI DAL

A variety of souring agents are added to this dal to ensure that it lives up to its name. It is a typical Hyderabadi dish much in demand by the locals.

Ingredients

½ cup split pigeon peas (arhar dal/
  toovar dal)
2 small tomatoes, chopped
12-15 curry leaves
¼ inch ginger, grated
3 garlic cloves, crushed
salt to taste
a pinch of turmeric powder
¼ teaspoon red chilli powder
½ teaspoon coriander seeds, powdered

2 teaspoons Tamarind Pulp (page 104)
2 tablespoons chopped fresh coriander
  leaves
2 green chillies, broken into 2-3 pieces

Seasoning
2 tablespoons pure ghee
6 garlic cloves
2 dried red chillies, broken in half
¼ teaspoon cumin seeds

Method

•   Pressure-cook the toovar dal in two and a half cups of water together with the tomatoes, half the curry leaves, the ginger and garlic till the pressure is released five times (five whistles). Remove the lid when the pressure has completely reduced and strain the dal through a sieve.

•   Bring the strained dal to a boil; add one cup of water, salt, turmeric powder, chilli powder and powdered coriander seeds and mix well. Add the tamarind pulp and cook over low heat for about ten minutes. Add the coriander leaves and green chillies and simmer for two or three minutes.

•   For the seasoning, heat the ghee in a pan; add the garlic, red chillies, cumin seeds and remaining curry leaves and sauté till fragrant. Pour the seasoning over the dal and cover immediately to trap the flavours. Serve hot with rice.

THIKRI KI DAL

'Thikri' means pieces of freshly broken earthenware pot which are used to season this unusual masoor dal dish.

Ingredients

1½ cups split red lentils (masoor dal)
salt to taste
½ tablespoon red chilli powder
¼ tablespoon turmeric powder
6 tablespoons pure ghee
1 large onion, sliced
4 green chillies, broken in half
2 tablespoons chopped fresh coriander
  leaves

1 teaspoon cumin seeds
4-5 dried red chillies
8-10 garlic cloves, chopped
¼ teaspoon fenugreek seeds (methi dana)
25 curry leaves
2 tablespoons lemon juice
2 three-inch pieces of earthenware (thikri)

Method

• Bring the lentils, salt and five cups of water to a boil. Remove the scum and add the chilli powder and turmeric powder. When half-cooked, add one tablespoon of ghee. Cook till the lentils are very soft and mash with the back of a ladle

• Heat three tablespoons of ghee in a pan and sauté the onion till golden brown. Add to the lentils with the green chillies and coriander leaves and cook for five minutes over low heat.

• Heat the remaining ghee in a small pan; add the cumin seeds, red chillies, garlic, fenugreek seeds and curry leaves. When the chillies begin to darken, pour the spices over the lentils and cover immediately to trap the flavours.

• Wash the thikri. Heat over burning charcoal or a flame till red hot. Place in the pan with the the lentils and cover the pan immediately. Just before serving remove the thikri and discard. Stir in the lemon juice and serve at once.

BAKARKHANI

Legend has it that this roti was the creation of Nawab Bakhar Khan, after whom it is named.

Ingredients

2 cups refined flour (maida)
½ teaspoon baking powder
salt to taste
¾ cup milk
2½ teaspoons sugar
1 tablespoon fresh yeast, crumbled

12-14 raisins (kishmish), optional
1 tablespoon chironji (charoli)
1 teaspoon kewra water
5 tablespoons pure ghee
10 almonds, blanched, peeled and sliced

Method

• Heat the milk and add the sugar; stir till the sugar dissolves. Dissolve the fresh yeast in a quarter cup of warm water and set aside. Soak the raisins and chironji in half a cup of warm water for five minutes, drain and set aside.

• Sift together the refined flour, baking powder and salt. Make a well in the centre and add the sweetened milk, a few drops of kewra water and the yeast; gradually mix into a soft dough. Cover with a damp cloth and set aside for ten minutes.

• Gradually incorporate three tablespoons of melted ghee into the dough. Add the almonds, raisins and chironji. Knead once again, cover and leave to stand in a warm place for thirty minutes to rise. Divide the risen dough into eight equal portions, shape into balls, cover and set aside for ten minutes.

• Preheat the oven to 240°C/475°F/Gas Mark 9.

• Flatten the balls of dough and roll them out into five-inch rounds. Prick the surface of each one with a fork and arrange on a baking tray. Bake for ten to twelve minutes. Remove from the oven, brush with ghee and serve hot.

Note: You need not grease the baking tray as the bakarkhani will release enough fat while baking. Do not use very hot water to dissolve yeast. The water should be lukewarm.

BIDARI PARANTHA

A version of the puffed puri, this parantha is a superb accompaniment to both vegetarian and non-vegetarian fare.

Ingredients

2 cups wholewheat flour (atta)
¾ cup refined flour (maida)
¼ cup semolina (sooji/rawa)

salt to taste
oil for deep-frying

Method

•   Sift the wholewheat flour and refined flour together. Mix in the semolina, salt and three-fourth cup of water and knead into a stiff dough. Cover with a damp cloth for twenty minutes.

•   Divide the dough into eight equal portions and shape into balls. Roll out each ball into a half-inch thick oval.

•   Heat the oil in a kadai and deep-fry the paranthas one by one over high heat until puffed up and light golden brown. Drain on absorbent paper and serve hot.

KACHCHE GOSHT KI BIRYANI

Raw marinated meat and steamed rice cooked in layers: the perfect presentation of an authentic Hyderabadi biryani.

Ingredients

1 kilogram mutton or lamb on the bone,
    cut into 2-inch pieces
2 cups basmati rice, soaked
2 two-inch pieces ginger
20-25 garlic cloves
½ cup fresh mint leaves
a few saffron threads
3 tablespoons milk
2 cups yogurt
2 green chillies, chopped
2 teaspoons red chilli powder
1 teaspoon turmeric powder
salt to taste
4-5 large onions, sliced and deep-fried
    till golden brown

5-6 cloves
1 inch cinnamon
5 green cardamoms
1 black cardamom
10 black peppercorns
¼ cup Potli Masala (page 104)
½ teaspoon caraway seeds (shahi jeera)
½ teaspoon green cardamom powder
2 teaspoons Garam Masala Powder (page 104)
½ cup chopped fresh coriander leaves
5 tablespoons pure ghee
2 tablespoons rose petals
1 teaspoon rose water
1 teaspoon kewra water
wholewheat flour (atta) dough to seal the pan

Method

•   Grind half the ginger and garlic to a fine paste. Cut the remaining ginger into fine strips. Chop half the mint leaves. Warm the milk slightly and soak the saffron in it.

•   In a bowl, mix together the mutton, yogurt, ginger-garlic paste, green chillies, chilli powder, turmeric powder, salt, one-third of the fried sliced onions and the chopped mint leaves. Leave to marinate for one hour.

•   Bring five cups of water to a boil in a separate pan. Place the cloves, cinnamon, green and black cardamoms, peppercorns and potli masala in a piece of muslin and tie up in a potli. Add the potli to the boiling water. Add salt to taste, the caraway seeds and soaked rice. Bring to a boil and cook till partially done. Drain.

•   Arrange half the marinated mutton in a thick-bottomed pan. Spread half the rice over the mutton. Top with one-third of the fried sliced onions and ginger strips. Sprinkle half the green cardamom powder, garam masala powder and coriander leaves on top. Roughly tear half the remaining mint leaves and sprinkle over the rice. Pour half the ghee over the layers.

•   Add half the saffron-flavoured milk to the pan. Sprinkle with half the rose petals, rose water and kewra water. Repeat the layers once again. Cover the pan and seal the lid with atta. Cook over a high heat for five minutes, then lower the heat. Place the pan on a tawa and cook over a low heat for forty-five minutes. Serve hot with raita.

QAABOOLI

This delectable rice dish gets its name from the word 'qaabooli' which means acceptance.

Ingredients

1¼ cups rice, soaked
½ cup split Bengal gram (chana dal), soaked
salt to taste
4-5 green cardamoms
2 one-inch sticks cinnamon
4-5 cloves
½ teaspoon turmeric powder
a pinch of saffron
2 tablespoons milk
2 tablespoons oil

½ teaspoon caraway seeds (shahi jeera)
½ tablespoon ginger-garlic paste
2-3 green chillies, chopped
5 onions, sliced and fried
1 teaspoon Garam Masala Powder (page 104)
1 tablespoon chopped fresh coriander leaves
½ cup yogurt
a few sprigs fresh mint leaves, roughly torn
2 tablespoons lemon juice

Method

• Drain rice and boil in three cups of water with salt and half the green cardamoms, cinnamon and cloves till almost done. Drain. Drain the chana dal and boil in one cup of water with salt and half the turmeric powder till just cooked. Soak the saffron in the milk.

• Heat the oil in a pan; add the remaining green cardamoms, cinnamon and cloves and sauté till fragrant. Add the caraway seeds and when they begin to sizzle, add the ginger-garlic paste and sauté for a few minutes. Add the green chillies and a small quantity of the fried onions. Add the cooked dal, the garam masala powder and coriander leaves and stir to mix well. Stir in the remaining turmeric powder and remove from heat. Add the yogurt and mix well.

• Transfer half the dal mixture into a separate pan. Spread half the rice over the dal and sprinkle with half the remaining fried onions, mint leaves, lemon juice and saffron. Spread the remaining dal over the rice followed by another layer of rice, fried onions, garam masala powder, mint leaves, lemon juice and saffron. Cover the pan tightly and cook on 'dum' for twenty to twenty-five minutes and serve hot.

SHEERMAL

'Sheer' means milk and 'mal' means riches. So Sheermal is a rich bread where the dough is kneaded with milk and kewra essence, brushed with saffron milk and baked to fragrant perfection.

Ingredients

2 cups refined flour (maida)
salt to taste
2 teaspoons sugar
¾ cup + 3 tablespoons milk

a few saffron threads
2-3 drops kewra essence
¼ cup pure ghee, melted
2 tablespoons butter + for greasing

Method

• Sift together the refined flour and salt. Dissolve the sugar in three-fourth cup of warm milk and the saffron in the remaining three tablespoons of warm milk.

• Add the sugar syrup and two or three drops of kewra essence to the flour and mix well. Add one-eighth cup of water and knead into a soft dough. Cover with a damp cloth and set aside for ten minutes. Add the ghee and knead it into the dough. Cover and set aside for ten minutes. Divide the dough into sixteen equal portions and shape into balls; cover and set aside for ten minutes.

• Preheat the oven to 240°C/475°F/Gas Mark 9. Flatten the balls on a lightly floured surface and roll out each ball into a six-inch round. Prick the surface with a fork. Grease a baking tray with butter, arrange the rounds on it and bake for five minutes. Remove from the oven, brush sheermals with the saffron and bake again for three or four minutes. Brush with butter and serve immediately.

SOFIYANI BIRYANI

Tender chicken cooked in royal almond masala layered with fragrant basmati rice. This is one biryani that would do any Hyderabadi khansama proud.

Ingredients

600 grams chicken on the bone, cut into
   1-inch pieces
1½ cups Basmati rice, soaked
12 green cardamoms
12 cloves
4 one-inch sticks cinnamon
1 cup yogurt, whisked
2 medium onions, sliced
2 tablespoons almond paste
1 tablespoon ginger paste

1 tablespoon garlic paste
2 tablespoons grated khoya/mawa
4 green chillies, cut into thin strips
salt to taste
1 teaspoon lemon juice
6 tablespoons pure ghee
1 tablespoon ginger-garlic paste
1 cup milk
1 teaspoon green cardamom powder
2 tablespoons cream

Method

• Place the chicken, six cardamoms, six cloves, two cinnamon sticks, the yogurt, onions, almond paste, ginger paste, garlic paste, khoya, green chillies, salt, lemon juice and two tablespoons of ghee in a deep pan. Cover and cook over a low heat till the chicken is tender.

• In a separate pan, add five cups of water, salt, ginger-garlic paste, remaining green cardamoms, remaining cloves and remaining cinnamon and bring to a boil. Add the rice and milk and cook till the rice is three-fourth done.

• Spread a layer of half the chicken in a pan. With a perforated spoon, layer half the rice over the chicken. Sprinkle half the cardamom powder and spread half the cream over the rice. Repeat the layers. Drizzle the remaining ghee around the edge of the pan. Cover and cook over a low heat for fifteen to twenty minutes. Serve hot.

DOUBLE KA MEETHA

Sliced bread, or as the Hyderabadis call it, 'double roti', is shallow-fried till golden and then baked with sugar syrup and condensed milk to make a spongy delicacy.

Ingredients

4 slices white bread
a pinch of saffron
2 teaspoons rose water
3½ tablespoons sugar
1 cup milk

3 tablespoons cream
2 tablespoons pure ghee
3-4 almonds, blanched and sliced
3-4 pistachios, sliced

Method

•   Soak the saffron in rose water. Make a thin syrup of sugar with two tablespoons of water and set aside. Boil the milk with the cream and simmer till it reduces to half its original quantity.

•   Preheat the oven to 180°C/350°F/Gas Mark 4. Remove the crusts from the bread and cut each slice in half diagonally to make two triangles. Heat the ghee in a pan and shallow-fry the bread slices till golden. Drain.

•   Dip the fried bread in sugar syrup and arrange on a baking tray. Pour the thickened milk over them. Top with almonds and pistachios. Sprinkle the saffron-rose water over and bake in the preheated oven for five or six minutes. Serve hot.

ASHARFIYON KA MEETHA

Almond pastry imprinted with a royal emblem - it simply melts in the mouth.

Ingredients

250 grams almonds
1⅓ cups sugar

a pinch of saffron
¼ teaspoon almond essence

Method

•   Blanch the almonds. Peel and grind to a fine paste with half a cup of water.

•   Place the paste in a handi, add the sugar and cook over a low heat, stirring continuously, till the mixture leaves the sides of the handi.

•   To test for doneness, drop a little mixture on a marble surface or a steel plate and leave to cool. It is ready if it does not stick to your fingers when you try to remove it.

•   Remove the mixture from the heat and set aside to cool. Mix the saffron in the almond essence and add to the mixture. Mix well. Divide the mixture into twenty-four portions. Press each portion between two asharfis (coins) so the sweets are imprinted with the designs of the coins.

KHUBANI KA MEETHA

'Khubani' is the Urdu word for dried apricots. Traditionally served at weddings, this sweet dish is made with apricot pulp topped with rich fresh cream: no shortcuts or substitutes like ice cream or custard will do!

Ingredients

500 grams dried apricots (khubani)   ¼ cup fresh malai (cream)
¾ cup sugar

Method

•   Soak the apricots in three cups of water overnight or for at least six hours. Remove the seeds and crack them open to remove the kernels. Blanch the kernels, remove the skin and set aside for garnishing.
•   Boil the apricots for ten minutes in the same water in which they were soaked. Add the sugar and continue to boil till the sugar dissolves. Remove from heat and cool slightly.
•   Reserve a few apricots and purée the rest. Cook the purée and the reserved whole apricots over a low heat for five to seven minutes. Serve, garnished with malai and apricot kernels.

GIL-E-FIRDAUS

'Gil-e-firdaus', literally translated is clay of paradise and this rich Hyderabadi kheer is paradise on a plate.

Ingredients

5 tablespoons raw rice   100 grams khoya/mawa, grated
250 grams bottle gourd (doodhi/lauki),   ½ cup sugar
  grated   a few drops of rose essence
2 tablespoons pure ghee   10 almonds, sliced
6 cups milk   a few rose petals

Method

•   Soak the rice for at least one hour. Drain and spread out to dry and grind coarsely.
•   Bring one cup of water to a boil in a pan and add the bottle gourd. Cook till soft, drain and set aside.
•   Heat the ghee in a deep pan; add the rice and sauté for a few seconds. Add the milk and bring to a boil. Lower heat and cook till the rice is soft. Add the bottle gourd and simmer for five minutes. Add the khoya and sugar and cook till the mixture is thick enough to coat the back of a spoon. Stir in the rose essence.
•   Pour into individual serving bowls and set aside to cool. Sprinkle sliced almonds and rose petals on top and serve chilled.

ANNEXURE

COCONUT CHUTNEY
Ingredients
- 1 cup grated fresh coconut
- salt to taste
- 1 tablespoon oil
- 1 dried red chilli, broken into 3 pieces
- ¼ teaspoon mustard seeds
- ½ teaspoon split black gram (dhuli urad dal)
- 5-6 curry leaves

Method
- Use only the white part of the grated coconut, discarding any brown bits.
- Grind coconut with very little water. Add salt to taste and mix well. The consistency of the chutney should be thick.
- Heat oil in a pan. Add broken red chillies, mustard seed and urad dal.
- When the seeds splutter and dal turns light brown, add curry leaves.
- Add the fried spices to the ground coconut. Mix thoroughly.

GREEN CHUTNEY
Ingredients
- 1 cup fresh coriander leaves
- ½ cup fresh mint leaves
- 2-3 green chillies
- black salt to taste
- ¼ teaspoon sugar
- 1 teaspoon lemon juice

Method
- Clean, wash and roughly chop coriander and mint leaves.
- Wash, remove seeds and chop green chillies.
- In a blender, process chopped coriander and mint leaves with chopped green chillies. Make a smooth paste using a little water if required.
- Add black salt and sugar.
- Transfer to a bowl and stir in the lemon juice.

GONGURA CHUTNEY

Ingredients

      1 bunch (250 grams) gongura (ambada) leaves
      3 tablespoons oil
      10 garlic cloves, chopped
      1½ teaspoons red chilli powder
      ½ teaspoon mustard seeds
      ½ teaspoon sesame seeds (til)
      ½ teaspoon roasted cumin powder
      ½ teaspoon coriander powder
      1 tablespoon Tamarind Pulp (page 104)
      Salt to taste

Method

- Heat two tablespoons of oil in a pan and sauté garlic till lightly browned. Add gongura leaves and continue to sauté for ten minutes.
- Heat the remaining oil in a separate pan and sauté the red chilli powder, mustard seeds, sesame seeds, roasted cumin powder and coriander powder for half a minute.
- Add the tamarind pulp and sautéed gongura leaves. Add half a cup of water and salt and cook till well mixed and the mixture is of a chutney consistency.
- Cool and store in an airtight jar.

TIL KI CHUTNEY

Ingredients

      100 grams sesame seeds (til)
      4 green chillies
      1½ tablespoons Tamarind Pulp (page 104)
      salt to taste
      3 tablespoons chopped fresh coriander leaves
      1 teaspoon oil
      ½ teaspoon split black gram (dhuli urad dal)
      3 dried red chillies, broken into bits
      ¼ teaspoon cumin seeds
      ¼ teaspoon mustard seeds
      6 curry leaves

Method

- Lightly roast the sesame seeds in a kadai and set aside to cool.
- Grind sesame seeds and green chillies to a coarse paste.
- Add tamarind pulp, salt and coriander leaves and mix well. Transfer the chutney to a bowl.
- Heat the oil in a pan, add urad dal, red chillies, cumin seeds, mustard seeds and curry leaves. When the mustard seeds begin to splutter, pour the sizzling spices over the ground paste and mix.

POTLI MASALA
Mix 200 grams coriander seeds, 25 grams sandalwood powder, 35 grams dried vetiver roots (khus), 35 grams bay leaves, 20 grams dried rose petals, 25 grams black cardamoms, 30 grams cassia buds, 15 grams cinnamon, 30 grams lichen/stone flower (patther phool), 35 grams kulanjan (paan ki jad) and 25 grams kapur kachri and store in an airtight jar. When required, tie a small amount in a piece of muslin and add it to the water to be used for cooking.

TAMARIND PULP
Soak 75 grams tamarind in 100 ml warm water for 10-15 minutes. Grind to a smooth paste and strain to remove any fibres. Store in an airtight container in the refrigerator.

NIHARI MASALA
Dry-roast till fragrant 4 tablespoons cumin seeds, 4 tablespoons fennel seeds, 12-15 whole dried red chillies, 2 tablespoons cloves, 5 green cardamoms, 3 black cardamoms, 25-30 black peppercorns, 4-5 tablespoons poppy seeds (khus khus), 2 bay leaves, 1 blade of mace, 2 tablespoons dried ginger powder (sonth), ½ tablespoon nutmeg powder and 4-5 cinnamon sticks. Add 4-5 tablespoons roasted chana dal powder. Remove from heat and set aside to cool. Grind to a fine powder. Sieve the mixture and store in the refrigerator in an airtight jar.

HYDERABADI GARAM MASALA POWDER
Dry-roast together 100 grams coriander seeds, 25 grams black cardamoms, 20 grams green cardamoms, 20 grams black peppercorns, 20 grams cloves, 20 grams cinnamon, 15 grams bay leaves, 10 grams cassia buds, 10 grams mace and 10 grams nutmeg over a low heat for 8-10 minutes or till fragrant. Cool and grind to a fine powder. When completely cold, store in an airtight container. Makes approximately 250 grams.

PopulaR prakashan
ROYAL HYDERABADI COOKING

PopulaR prakashan
ROYAL HYDERABADI COOKING

PopulaR prakashan
ROYAL HYDERABADI COOKING

PopulaR prakashan
ROYAL HYDERABADI COOKING

PopulaR prakashan
ROYAL HYDERABADI COOKING

PopulaR prakashan
ROYAL HYDERABADI COOKING

PopulaR prakashan
ROYAL HYDERABADI COOKING

PopulaR prakashan
ROYAL HYDERABADI COOKING

PopulaR prakashan
ROYAL HYDERABADI COOKING

PopulaR prakashan
ROYAL HYDERABADI COOKING

PopulaR prakashan
ROYAL HYDERABADI COOKING

PopulaR prakashan
ROYAL HYDERABADI COOKING

PopulaR prakashan
ROYAL HYDERABADI COOKING

PopulaR prakashan
ROYAL HYDERABADI COOKING

PopulaR prakashan
ROYAL HYDERABADI COOKING

PopulaR prakashan
ROYAL HYDERABADI COOKING

PopulaR prakashan
ROYAL HYDERABADI COOKING

PopulaR prakashan
ROYAL HYDERABADI COOKING

PopulaR prakashan
ROYAL HYDERABADI COOKING

PopulaR prakashan
ROYAL HYDERABADI COOKING

PopulaR prakashan
ROYAL HYDERABADI COOKING

PopulaR prakashan
ROYAL HYDERABADI COOKING

PopulaR prakashan
ROYAL HYDERABADI COOKING

PopulaR prakashan
ROYAL HYDERABADI COOKING

PopulaR prakashan
ROYAL HYDERABADI COOKING

PopulaR prakashan
ROYAL HYDERABADI COOKING

PopulaR prakashan
ROYAL HYDERABADI COOKING

PopulaR prakashan
ROYAL HYDERABADI COOKING

PopulaR prakashan
ROYAL HYDERABADI COOKING

PopulaR prakashan
ROYAL HYDERABADI COOKING

PopulaR prakashan
ROYAL HYDERABADI COOKING

PopulaR prakashan
ROYAL HYDERABADI COOKING

PopulaR prakashan
ROYAL HYDERABADI COOKING

PopulaR prakashan
ROYAL HYDERABADI COOKING

PopulaR prakashan
ROYAL HYDERABADI COOKING

PopulaR prakashan
ROYAL HYDERABADI COOKING

PopulaR prakashan
ROYAL HYDERABADI COOKING

PopulaR prakashan
ROYAL HYDERABADI COOKING

PopulaR prakashan
ROYAL HYDERABADI COOKING

PopulaR prakashan
ROYAL HYDERABADI COOKING

PopulaR prakashan
ROYAL HYDERABADI COOKING

PopulaR prakashan
ROYAL HYDERABADI COOKING

PopulaR prakashan
ROYAL HYDERABADI COOKING

PopulaR prakashan
ROYAL HYDERABADI COOKING

PopulaR prakashan
ROYAL HYDERABADI COOKING

PopulaR prakashan
HYDERABADI COOKING

PopulaR prakashan
HYDERABADI COOKING

PopulaR prakashan
HYDERABADI COOKING

PopulaR prakashan
HYDERABADI COOKING

PopulaR prakashan
HYDERABADI COOKING